Porch Poems

Susanna Connelly Holstein,
Cheryl Denise, Kirk Judd,
Sherrell Runnion Wigal

Sheila-Na-Gig Editions

Porch Poems © Kirk Judd, 2023
Cover Photo: Kirk Judd
Back Cover Photo: Larry Holstein

ISBN: 9798987305874

Sheila-Na-Gig Editions
Russell, KY
Hayley Mitchell Haugen, Editor
www.sheilanagigblog.com

Praise for *Porch Poems*

Porch Poems is an ars poetica that invokes the great tradition of "porch sitting," in which we are invited to sit with four of West Virginia's best known and most beloved poets. These are poems that last, full of the natural world, made especially for those moments when time slows to a stop. These poets are the keepers of mysteries and wonder, and their poems burn with imagination as they move with ease between the borders of the past and future.

—Renée K. Nicholson, Director, WVU Humanities Center
author of *Roundabout Directions to Lincoln Center* and *Fierce and Delicate*

Some of my cherished memories are of my family sitting on porches and in breezeways to talk about all kinds of things—how the garden was coming along, how the neighbor was handling some new scandal or tragedy, how quickly we kids were growing. Sometimes, some of the family would drag out their mandolins, fiddles, and banjos and play bluegrass music. The poems in this book remind me of those times. These writers get at the heart of what it means to be blessed with the stories and experiences of life in West Virginia. These poems are the tangled strands of "DNA" that make up every rural, suburban, and urban dweller in the state. While reading these verses, I could hear every bird, feel every breeze, and smell every aroma swept over the hills and streams of my childhood home. When I let these words wash over me, I feel as though time is standing still, giving me a chance to wonder at the profound and striking moments offered in these pages.

—David B. Prather, author of *We Were Birds*

"The Spirit Rising from Everything" (Judd) is here in *Porch Poems*, from Wigal's childhood of scarcity to her at-oneness with nature: forsythia shouting "yellow hallelujahs", "twice-fallen rain" dripping from leaves; from Holstein's struggling humans, their needs, their uneasy alliances with nature and animals, with the living and the dead; from Denise's tumult, gassing it down the QEW away from memories of the past to a new life, reconsidering everything; from Judd's love of the world, of family and friends, from his loyalty, saying while a storm brews, "I could not/not come with you." Readers, enjoy!

—Sandy Vrana, Professor of Literature and Writing (retired)
Alderson Broaddus University

For Barbara Smith

Ecology: the branch of biology dealing with the relations and interactions between organisms and their environment, including other organisms

The sound of the breeze
The smell of horned owls
The smile of blackberries
The sweetness of rocks
The pull of the ocean
The voice of God

From "Improved Definitions"
Barbara Smith

Table of Contents

Foreword

In May 2016, four poets met at a camp in Buckeye in Pocahontas County, West Virginia. The camp is the old Section Foreman's house built in the early 1900's when the 101 mile long Greenbrier Railroad was constructed along the Greenbrier River from the town of Cass on the northern end to Caldwell in the south. The railroad hauled millions of board feet of lumber out of Pocahontas County until it ceased operations in the 1970's. Over 80 miles of the right-of-way became the Greenbrier River Trail, a very popular hiking and biking destination. The front porch of the camp actually sits on that right-of-way. And that porch is where most of the poems in this volume were conceived, written, edited, discussed, edited some more, rejected, discussed some more, edited some more, and finally emerged as finished pieces.

Each of us, Cheryl Denise of Barbour County, Susanna Connelly Holstein of Jackson County, Kirk Judd of Monongalia County, and Sherrell Runnion Wigal of Wood County, are long-established writers and have attended and conducted many creative writing workshops around the state, but we wanted to take a deeper and more reflective dive into our own work. We decided to continue to meet for at least one weekend a year at what we were calling Poet Camp. Since we all knew each other very well, and respected each other's work and judgment, there was an element of safety and trust that fostered an excellent environment for creating poetry. But that didn't mean it wasn't tough. We scrutinized each poem, each thought, each idea, each line, each word, and each syllable (spoken and unspoken) and decomposed and recomposed them until we and the poems were exhausted.

It was all poetry, all the time, except for cooking and doing dishes and evening campfires under brilliant stars in the company of owls and coyotes. We shared poetry on the back porch, on the front porch, on the porch swing and everywhere in between while watching hawks and eagles and other wildlife and listening to the silence and beauty of Pocahontas County. And we wrote. And wrote.

In 2022, we decided to put together this chapbook of some of the work produced there at Poet Camp. Each poet contributed 6 pieces connected to the experience, with the idea that they would select 5 apiece for a 20 poem volume. That didn't work. All 24 poems are included. Nothing missed the cut. And because they are so intimate and interconnected, we decided not to attribute the poems individually, but to simply list the poems and authors in the back of the book. It seemed to be the right way.

So here this is. *Porch Poems* by the *Porch Poets* created at *Poet Camp* in one of the most beautiful and peaceful spots in Pocahontas County, which is one of the most beautiful and peaceful spots in West Virginia, which is one of the most beautiful and peaceful spots on the planet. We hope the book brings you some of that beauty and peace.

Audience Blessing

Blessings to each of you.
May you find something familiar
in the words we share.
May you find kindness.
May you find solace.
May you remember
one moment you had forgotten.
May you find a gentle way
to listen to the morning
gossip of crows.

Things You Can Only See If You're Not Looking

A lark's condensed breath
As it sings a too-cool morning into day

The star next to the star
You think is Alnilam
Sparkling in The Hunter's belt
Low in the November sky

Your lover's hand reaching
Just before it touches your shoulder

Ghost cats

The infinte grace
Of the first raindrop

Green knowing it will be yellow
In February forsythia

Owls at night

Mars winking
Jupiter too
And Saturn
Venus with both eyes

The corpse's smile
Just before you pass

The tear you never cried

The last pin oak leaf as it falls
The soundwave it makes

Squirrels in a beech grove

The bend in the tail of the comet

The animal no one has ever seen

Sleep

The first purple redbud

The rise of trout downstream from your cast

Cedar Waxwings eating the last cherries

The color of the devil's eye

Your mother's last breath

The spirit rising from everything
From you
From the river
From the grass blade and the elk
From the sentient wolf
And sheep in the pasture
From hay in the field
From peaches in the orchard
From turtles in the pond

The swell and pull of it all
Lifting, lifting, lifting

The Day Before

Morning is warm bed and cold floor.

Bacon.
Words spoken and unspoken
Move around and through.

Daylight warms the porch,
The pasture,
The book in your hands.

Poet says "Light is ivory."
You smile.
Poets know light has color.

Afternoon is cut grass and gasoline,
Sweat, high sun.
Clouds lean down.
Shadows play.
Birds laugh and move on.

Poems float in rising air.
Hawks hover above them,
Devour them
Like the day devours you.

It is easy to sit on the swing
Wait for friends
You know will come.

Blue unburdens the sky
Deeper and deeper
In low slant light

Of early October evening.
Things settle.
Birds.
Daylight.
Words.
You.

In gentle fields
Buck deer browse unhurried.
Poems fall down,
Lead you past the ridge
Toward planets rising,
Moon following across
Unrhymed clouds.

The book,
Still open,
Trembles.

Night wanders in,
Sits on the swing beside you,
Sighs.

Last Night the Mockingbird

and now, black-capped chickadee, crow,
brown thrasher, dove,
all those glorious birds of dawn.

Here is rabbit, gray squirrel,
towhee demands "drink-your-tea"
as steam rises from blue mugs.

Across green meadow, on a hollow tree,
red-bellied woodpecker
rat-a-tats his territorial drumming.

Along the Greenbrier River,
wood ducks fly upstream,
Canada geese down.

What more can we say
about this morning
that hasn't already been said

by riotous fence-line forsythia
as it shouts yellow hallelujahs
into the blossom of light?

Poetry Before Breakfast

In that wavery time after waking
before the ordinary day begins,
I write.

My good dog, who smells like the woods,
lies on his yellow-grey back
stretching impossibly long
as I scratch his belly.

For warm up I read Steve Scafidi's
poem "The Egg Suckers,"
then Jeff Gundy's
"Astonishing Details of the Universe."
While I write, Paul Simon sings me to Graceland
and my English Breakfast Tea with cream
steams the morning.

In grade school I chewed my hair
pretending no one could see me.

The damp taste of fear has gone now
and my thoughts don't halt and stutter
but rise sure as the sun.

A voice flows through me:
Will you go further?
This is not an accusation,
not a direction.

Yes, I answer.

Stopped Clock

Why do you look at me
over and over?
It is always ten minutes until eleven.
It is where I chose to stop.

I watch you hurry,
watch your faces push ahead
as if to see more than what there is,
but here I stay,
where time stands still.

Why do you not stop,
be calm,
listen for a change?
All your hurry brings you to this,
to look at me and see
it is still ten minutes until eleven.

Nothing much has changed,
children are born,
people fall in love,
men plan wars,
bluebird builds his nest
in the same fencepost,
sings the same songs.

The world will spin and spin
but always come back to here,
ten minutes until eleven,
so I can wait,
I can watch and know
you will all be here again.

You will strive, struggle,
laugh, lose, create, destroy.
In the end your hands,
like mine, will stop.

I tell you, before that time comes,
to seek the solace of quiet,
the serenity of silence.
Look into your own face
instead of mine.

Apples

The tree needs no
clock or calendar.

Accepts all,
drought, rain,
war, hungry bear,
seasonal tilt and turn.

In September
its baring branches jewel.
With or without me
one by one
apples
relax,
       release,
             fall

sacred and sweet.

Blue Watering Can

In her front yard, a peach tree heavy with fruit,
around its base a tractor tire filled with ditch dirt
where she plants tomatoes,
waters them with a blue watering can.

Cigarette smoke hovers,
long silver hair drifts in wisps to her waist.
More Winstons and matches
wait in the pocket of her cotton apron.

When the watering is done she sits
in a wooden rocker on the porch
built on to the trailer,
finishes her smoke with long, slow drags,
making it last,
making it last.

Over the hill
coonhounds shift sadly on long chains.
One jumps to the roof of his doghouse,
as if to better see the road, the trailer,
the man inside who wheezes
with the steady beat of the oxygen tank,
watches hunting shows on TV,
as if maybe one night he will unchain the dogs,
grab his gun, walk the midnight hills again.

She waits in the rocker, puffs blue billows,
looks at the tree, the tomatoes, the road,
at nothing and everything,
one day after another.

She watches the peaches swell,
the tomatoes redden and ripen,

listens
to the steady hiss of oxygen.

Reprieve

In a stained gingham apron
she stands in the kitchen doorway,
sips from a heavy white mug
the first of the day's brown brew.

By the clothesline, raucous crows bring news
in a language she does not understand.
Their noise startles movement beneath a bush,
a frightened rabbit leaps
toward the garden of blue-gray cabbage,
lime-green lettuce standing in orderly rows.

At the fence
hummingbirds whir their wings,
dart and dive through trumpet vines.
Fog lifts from dewy grass,
sun sparkles on ripe strawberries.

Clouds move in,
hides the sun's bright promise.
She sees, but knows there will be no rain
since the dew is heavy
and the wind is from the south.
She pulls on a pink cardigan,
fastens its one remaining button,
takes the egg basket
from a hook by the door.

The rooster struts and crows,
the hens fuss and worry.
One, draggled and feather-worn,
sits on a nest.

"So you're laying again, old girl."
The woman reaches in,
finds a warm brown egg.
"Guess I won't be gettin' the hatchet today."

The clouds move on.
"This will be a good day," she says.
Sunlight gleams
on the sharp edge of the blade
hanging just inside the henhouse door.

The Keeper

There is a light in the window
of the homeplace. No one notices.
No one cares.
No one sees the old one,
keeper of mysteries,
seer of futures.

No footprints trace her path,
but the cat raises his hackles,
hisses wide-eyed at her passing shadow.
She whispers secrets to red butterflies,
knows the shrouds in heaven's basement,
mysteries stored in the attics of hell.
She sees where the dead walk,
hears the singing of the yet unborn.

Around her gate sweet honeysuckle twines,
lavender and bergamot,
rue and cow's parsley mingle.
Herbs for goodness, herbs for evil,
who can know what makes her tea?

She keeps the kettle steaming on the fire,
bread, butter, honey on her table
for company not yet devoured by death or life.

Within her house of bones there beats
a heart, patched with sinew, sewn with gut.
She listens to voices from murmuring graves;
the sorrow of the world butters her bread.
Over it all she pours sweet honey,
tends the light.

Heritage

The mother's a washing machine brimming
with cucumbers, a table crowded with mason jars
and pickling spices.

She's the hum of the needle
making costumes for her children's Ice Carnival.

She's a china teapot,
a slice of grape pie.

The daughter is the dare covering the eyes
of a boy playing chicken on the fast road,

the crimson tip of a cigarette
nestled in the oak
watching church boys play football.

She's the quiet wash of a cross-country sunrise,
running to be alone.

The mother struggled in high school,
dropped out, worked at Wally & Llyod's
gave up wages for family groceries,
siblings' college funds.

When the daughter becomes ill with doubt
at nursing school, the mother recognizes the demons,
takes her out for bagels Monday mornings,
tells her she's proud of her for making it this far.

At twenty-two the daughter flies away
to volunteer in a dusty Colorado town.

As a public health nurse so much is expected
she thinks she might break.
She blames God
and starts writing.

The mother, who'd been to the hospital
when her own mind jammed up,
knows what to slip off and when.
She reads the poems, understands.

When one appears in the church bulletin
she tells everyone her daughter is a famous poet.

The mother is a lilac bush, a sweet lullaby.

At night the daughter's room fills with the fragrant faraway song.

DNA

His father was firewood
His mother the ax.
He knows how to burn.

His grandfather was a porch
His grandmother a bicycle.
When he rests, he still moves.

His uncle is a lilac
Another a fence post.
He has boundaries around his blooms.

His brother is a leaf
His sister the sky.
He picks up the fallen in the open.

His father was a moon
His mother a hawk.
He hunts at night.

His grandfather was a trail
His grandmother a boot.
He travels light and fast.

His uncle is a hemlock
Another a spade.
He is green and planted.

His brother is tea
His sister breakfast.
He prepares his own meals.

His father was grass
His mother a scythe.
He has been cut down.

His father was a sparrow
His mother a jay.
He is a flock.

What We Had

We lived up Steele Holler
where fences were
only barriers for cattle,
no real "ours" or "theirs,"

red linoleum counter tops,
green used carpet
from the funeral home,
wall-to-wall
in each small bedroom,

free gas,
space heaters,
a spring by the driveway,
later a drilled well,
later still running water,

two working parents,
butter and sugar sandwiches
the last week of the month,
free-range summers
minus morning and garden chores,

Dad puttering on Sundays
making magic from bushel
baskets of parts, oily rags,
crescent wrenches.

Not yet knowing there would come
books spilling with words.
Nouns we'd string on invisible wire,
wear as necklaces,

dangle from our hair.
Verbs filling acres and acres,
crossing county lines, state lines,
floating up and down rivers,
winging across oceans and icebergs,
lifting into unimaginable galaxies.

Words to carry us far
yet always tethered,
umbilical pull,
to 7.3 acres of dirt-scraped earth,
lung-deep scent of cows,
a pile of stained white work-rags.

The Rusty Spoon

*"Why do you keep it," she asked, "like it's something special,
an ornament or a treasure? It's just a rusty spoon."*

She didn't know his eyes,
glimmering blue, sharp as ice needles.
She didn't see his skin,
worn and weathered,
craggy with years and hard use,
hear his voice, smoke-darkened, prison rough.
She didn't smell the sharp acid of oak
or his sweat from splitting a mountain
of winter warmth.
She didn't feel the tough leather of his hands,
split, callused, nails bitten to the quick.

She didn't know the story,
how he found the spoon
two feet down in red clay, digging a grave
in a churchyard with markers so old
the names were worn away.
She didn't see his cabin,
tucked under the edge of a laurel thicket
hidden beside a dark stream.
She didn't hear the wonder in his voice,
see the mystery in his eyes
as he handed it to me.

Rules for the Open Mic Poetry Reading

FOR THE POET

Don't explain the whole poem before you begin.

Don't mumble or slouch
or pick the scab at your elbow.

Don't apologize.
Don't fret like a preschooler searching for Mom.

If you think you're Frost or Dickinson
then go ahead read the first draft
you wrote this morning.

Tepid clapping is not permission
for you to read another half hour.

No sermons.

No more than two unrequited loves.

And please no perineum or vagina poems.

No fake British accent.

Your poem is not so significant
you need to crescendo every line,
nor so deep as to warrant a sloth's pace.

Never fade out in the final stanza
or mute the last word.

If you fail, fail gloriously.

Treat poetry with respect.
Don a clean shirt;
read as if you LIKE your poems.

FOR THE LISTENER

Don't make grocery lists
or play solitaire on your phone.

Focus on the reader
not your dirty nails.

Don't be afraid to sigh, nod, hoot.

Drink beer if it makes listening easier.

Gaze out the window of your mind
and change what you see according to what you hear.

Allow yourself to be surprised.

Afterwards don't rush off.
Discuss a poem over wine and cheese.

If you have the means, buy a book you like.

Instead of listening to the radio
on the way home, try to remember a metaphor.

Next time bring a friend,
come early, lounge near the front.
Smile at the reader before she begins.
Let the poem lead you where it will.

Nuisance Poets

Section 10.23

West Virginia Linguistic Management Regulations 2021

Poets committing depredations upon academic or small press anthologies, independent press chapbooks, ezines, or regional literary publications, instigating live readings at libraries or general public gatherings, or when concentrated at conferences or workshops so as to constitute a hazard and/or other nuisance may be taken at any time.

<u>No daily limits.</u>

A Blessing for Poets

May a poem find you before breakfast.

May the bees forever make honey for your tea.
     May it stay warm
          while you refine the last line.

May you never fear the quiet,
     the empty page,
     your reader,
     your brother,
     the editor.
     Rejection will come; don't mope all day.

Write your truth,
lose control,
keep your hand moving.

Invite the muse
     though she's torn
          a thousand invitations.

Kiss your internal censor goodnight,
keep him asleep
until the third draft.

Recite your poems to your dog,
your lover, the neighbor,
the purple-haired cashier at the grocery store.

Call your grandma.
If you have none, find one.
There are always old women keeping the fire.

Slip into the sacred ritual
you and the words
as it was in the beginning
when you found yourself lonely
in bed, with a pen and a notebook.

Twice Fallen Rain

Beyond the front porch,
evening hangs silent
except twice-fallen rain
as it drops from leaf to leaf.

The storm, now 30 miles away,
still its lightning calls and calls,
strikes a resplendent ochre sunset.

Black snake glides toward the river.
Twenty feet away, a large doe
crunches small, green apples
left by wind.

Owls come silent,
insistent, almost invisible.
Four fledglings who stay for days.

Beneath hedgerow
glow worms
burn with imagination.

Storm Warning

Beware, weary travelers,
your way will not be easy;
there will be rivers of tears,
broken bridges of promises,
ragged holes of misery.

Be brave.
Know the power of God,
the strength of your heart,
and with your stout stick of resolve
travel on.

Ahead there is light, and peace,
a great laughing river in which to wash
the dirt of the road from your body,
the dust of despair from your soul.

What Sustains Me

The long line of horse-and-buggies
that clip-clop to church Sunday mornings
sound like tree frogs on the hillside.

Red-tails riding thermals while four poets
on the porch prune their metaphors.

Mom's bearhug and laughter when I was a girl,
when I asked why Grandpa, normally happy,
yelled when he preached, madly shaking his fist.

The bright pompoms tying the black shawls
of Old Order women, that one autumn
when they were allowed a dollop of color:
lime green, McIntosh red,
orange, fuchsia and turquoise.

An old dog asleep in a sunbeam.

The Indian tribe that says all creation stories are true.

The bearded man who says many creation stories
start with revenge, battles, and poison,
but ours starts with a word, a breath.

The Egyptian prof who buys a lamb to remember
Abraham's willingness to sacrifice his son.
He chooses our best,
binds the lamb's legs with electrical tape,
gently heaves him into the trunk of his BMW.

Early morning fog rolling off the pond.

My husband who turns the sanctuary into a woodshop.
For Sunday worship we build houses for barred owls.

My 105-year-old Grandma
in her apartment
singing hymns.

Borders

At the border between past and future
no caution sign advises slippery roads ahead,
slow down, make a U-turn when safe.
No rheumy-eyed cop waits at Wagner's Corner
cocks his head through the window and warns:

>   *You know when you come back*
>   *everything's going to be the same*
>   *but you'll feel like a traitor.*

But already you've gassed it down the QEW
along with all the other jalopies, hotrods & minivans—
three lanes of traffic, horns, exhaust fumes.
Tractor trailers block signs for off ramps:
you couldn't change course if you tried.

You crest the Sky Bridge,
a new horizon beckons
like a lost friend you never had
and you think, surely, she will help you find yourself.

So you ignore the final duty-free shop
stuffed with maple leaf souvenirs you'll want later.
And now you wait in line
while that German Shepherd that lunged at you as a kid
circles your rusty Toyota.

Then suddenly Carl, the bully from grade two
bounds out of a booth: *Anything to declare?*
You want to say your freedom, a sovereign mind;
but a joke could send you back
to your childhood.

And now you're winding up a gravel road
living on a community farm,
chasing sheep, raising chicks,
fixing poetry in the college basement
with an English prof, a cross-dresser,
and a preacher who writes science fiction.

It bothers you that people here
leave their shoes on in the house,
admit they're hungry when asked only once,
that no one makes butter tarts
or goes curling Friday nights.

Years pass: still some days you ache
for walks that lead to your sister's flowerbeds.

When you hear plans for the new arena
you dream of an invitation to come home,
read your hockey poem.
Your old schoolmates will stomp and howl.

You imagine all they remember
is the girl who failed grade two,
who later rinsed diapers in the hopper
at the nursing home when it seemed
everyone else was a rising Malcolm Gladwell.

But even though you unfurled and became bold,
reading poems on the radio,
still some days, roaming these hills,
you wish for a family crisis,
an unexpected surgery,

anything to pull you north for a month,
maybe two,
pretending you could stay.

Almost Hidden

We walked
hand in hand at first,
later single file,
first me leading
then you,
on the single track
farther and farther
from the road,

deeper into the sparse wood
toward the full bend
in the Mississippi,

a wide, big-bodied river here
in the belly of the nation
splitting the country
North to South,

a road map for the
splendid migrations,
hundreds of thousands
moving ahead of the seasons,
toward or away from
toward or away from
feeding
breeding
birth
death.

It is too far to walk,
they told us in town,
on a day

when a storm is coming,
but you could not come here
without seeing
and I could not
not come with you.

So, after hours
getting colder and weary
with clothes and boots wet
from flakes on the outside
and sweat on the inside,
we broke out of the wood,
crossed the sand hills
down the river's bank,

steam rising from our faces
and from the wetlands
flanking both sides of the path
we stopped
at the top of a rise
and looked down.

I saw your eyes
and knew why
we had come
here
now
to see the cranes
standing
thousands
still and patient
breathing
quiet
almost hidden
in the morning snow.

Composition

Of the gravel in the road
Of the smooth rocks in the stream
Of the lichen on the banks
Of the squirrel's nest in the tree

Of the moonshine in the jar
Of the sunshine on the hill
Of the fox track in the sand
Of the sawdust in the mill

Of the coal inside the fire
Of the water in the spring
Of the stars above the sky
Of the blackbird's bloodied wing

Of the warmth inside my bed
Of the touch of your cool hand
Of the iron under the bridge
Of the losing of this land

Of the trout in Laurel Run
Of the yellow flower's hue
Of the grass under my feet
Of the years I've had with you

Of the apple-blossomed air
Of the baby in my arms
Of the berries on the vine
Of the telling of the yarn

Of the roads that ever go
Of the eagle's lofty flight
Of the travels yet to come
Of the day and of the night

Of the music of the earth
Of the music of the wind
Of the time that stays forever
Of the end when it begins

Fermata

There is one pause,
        a spontaneous moment,
when evening lays itself down.

        Wind holds its breath.
        Birds settle—silence their songs.
        Animals freeze.
        Long out-breath of grasses.

Then,
        a blue inhale,
        tenderness of evening slips in on cooler air.

Night approaches.
        Hermit Thrush rushes into song.
        Doe and fawn rise in meadows.
        Snakes slide home.
        Dusk pulls near.

Patient on the porch
        I wait alone for that succinct moment

my body relaxes,
        skin marries the air.

Poems and Poets

Cheryl's poems:
Poetry Before Breakfast, Heritage, Rules for the Open Mic Poetry Reading, A Blessing for Poets, What Sustains Me, Borders

Susanna's poems:
Stopped Clock, Blue Watering Can, Reprieve, The Keeper, The Rusty Spoon, Storm Warning

Kirk's poems:
Things You Can Only See If You're Not Looking, The Day Before, DNA, Nuisance Poets, Almost Hidden, Composition

Sherrell's poems:
Audience Blessing, Last Night the Mockingbird, Apples, What We Had, Twice Fallen Rain, Fermata

Acknowledgments

Cheryl Denise: *Fences* (Cascadia Publishing House, Dream-Seeker Poetry Series, Telford, PA,2022): "A Blessing for Poets," "Borders," "Poetry Before Breakfast," "What Sustains Me"

Kirk Judd: *The Northern Appalachia Review:* "DNA," "Nuisance Poets," "The Day Before," "Things You Can Only See If You're Not Looking"

Sherrell Wigal: *Women Speak:* "Fermata"

The poets would like to thank Sheila-Na-Gig Editions and publisher Hayley Mitchell Haugen for help in making this book possible. Long-time friend and fellow poet Wilma Acree provided excellent and valuable proofreading input. To all the poetry workshop leaders, poets who attend those workshops, writing retreat and conference directors, and all those who support the birthing of poems into this world, we send our sincere thanks.

Biographical Notes

Cheryl Denise grew up in Elmira, Ontario. She went to the red brick Mennonite church beside the white clapboard Old Order Meetinghouse. After nursing school, she went into Voluntary Service and worked as a public health nurse in La Jara, Colorado. She fell for her future husband while helping to make suppers at the Homeless Shelter where he was volunteering. Now they live in the intentional community of Shepherds Field, near Philippi, WV, in a timber framed home they built when they were young and brimming with energy. Cheryl is the author of the poetry books, "Fences" (2022), "What's in the Blood" (2012), and "I Saw God Dancing" (2005), all published by Cascadia Publishing House, DreamSeeker Books, Telford, PA. She has a spoken word poetry CD, "Leaving Eden" (2012) available on Amazon. She enjoys hiking, canoeing, biking, and cross-country skiing with her husband, Mike Miller. Visit her on Facebook at Cheryl Denise, poet.

Susanna Connelly Holstein's work has appeared in the poetry anthologies "Fed From the Blade" (Woodland Press), "Voices on Unity: Coming Together, Falling Apart" and "Diner Stories" (Mountain State Press) as well as in short story anthologies and online journals. She was a columnist for 10 years for the regional magazine "Two-Lane Livin'" and has been blogging since 2007. A traditional storyteller and ballad singer, Susanna has performed for national venues and to audiences across West Virginia. In 2015 Susanna was named a West Virginia History Hero. When not writing or performing, she sells antiques and works in her gardens in Jackson County.

Kirk Judd, founding member of West Virginia Writers, Inc., has lived, worked, trout fished and wandered around in West Virginia all his life. Kirk was a member of the Appalachian Literary League, a former president (and JUG recipient) of West Virginia Writers, Inc., and is a founding member of and creative writing instructor for Allegheny Echoes, Inc., dedicated to the support and preservation of WV cultural heritage arts. Author of 3 collections of poetry "Field of Vision" (1986), "Tao-Billy" (1996), and "My People Was Music" (2014), and a co-editor of the widely acclaimed anthology, "Wild, Sweet Notes – 50 Years of West Virginia Poetry 1950 – 1999", he is widely published. He has been featured three times on American Public Radio on *"The Poet and The Poem"* with WV native Grace Cavalieri and has appeared on the acclaimed public radio show *Mountain Stage.* Kirk was honored to be one of 5 readers selected for the installation ceremony of Louise McNeill Pease as WV Poet Laureate in 1979. He is internationally known for his performance work combining poetry and old-time music and has performed poetry in Ireland and across West Virginia at fairs, concerts, and festivals since the 1970s.

Sherrell Runnion Wigal is a poet originally from Roane County, West Virginia, now living in Wood County. In past years she served as director of the West Virginia Writers' annual writers conference and has been the past coordinator of the literary events tent at the West Virginia State Folk Festival. She conducts numerous creative writing workshops throughout the area. Sherrell has presented her work throughout West Virginia and surrounding states. Her list of performances includes the Arthur Brandon Humanities Lecture series at Alderson-Broaddus College, the Rhythm and Rhyme series at Kanawha County Public Library, the annual Vandalia Gathering and the Stonewall Jackson Jubilee. Her writing appears in many publications throughout the country. Much of Sherrell's poetry reflects her love, appreciation and connection to nature, people and the cultural heritage of West Virginia.